All of a sudden Too-Tall lashed
out. He hit Ferdy smack in the chest. Ferdy
went flying backward over Skuzz.

Ferdy picked himself up. He clenched his
small fists at his sides. "Give me my book!"
he yelled in a high voice. But another gang
member was already kneeling behind him.
Too-Tall simply pushed Ferdy to the
ground again. The whole gang roared with
laughter.

BIG CHAPTER BOOKS

The Berenstain Bears and the Drug Free Zone

The Berenstain Bears and the New Girl in Town

The Berenstain Bears Gotta Dance!

The Berenstain Bears and the Nerdy Nephew

Coming soon

The Berenstain Bears Accept No Substitutes

The Berenstain Bears and the Female Fullback

The Berenstain Bears and the Red-Handed Thief

The Berenstain Bears
and the Wheelchair Commando

The Berenstain Bears and the Nerdy Nephew

By Stan & Jan Berenstain

A BIG CHAPTER BOOK™

Random House 🏠 New York

Library of Congress Cataloging-in-Publication Data
Berenstain, Stan.
The Berenstain Bears and the nerdy nephew /
by Stan & Jan Berenstain.
    p. cm. — (A Big chapter book)
SUMMARY: Brother and Sister Bear don't realize the problems
they will face when they agree to help Professor Actual Factual's
super-smart nephew fit in at school.
ISBN 0-679-83610-1 (pbk.). — ISBN 0-679-93610-6 (lib. bdg.)
[1. Schools—Fiction. 2. Behavior—Fiction. 3. Bears—Fiction.]
I. Berenstain, Jan. II. Title. III. Series. IV. Series:
Berenstain, Stan. Big chapter book.
PZ7.B4483Bejn 1993   92-32564
[Fic]—dc20

Manufactured in the United States of America 10 9 8 7 6 5 4

BIG CHAPTER BOOKS is a trademark of Berenstain Enterprises, Inc.

Contents

Chapter 1
New Cub in Town

One fall evening, as the sun set and the
moon rose over the Bear family's tree house,
the Bears were gathered in the living room.
Each was doing something different. Mama
sat on the sofa going through the week's
expenses. Sister had her schoolbooks spread
out on the floor and was doing homework.
Both had half an ear tuned in to what was
going on between Papa and Brother. That

seemed much more interesting. Papa sat in his big easy chair. He was looking at a math test that Brother had brought home for him to sign.

"C-minus isn't up to your standard, Son," Papa said with a frown. "You're usually pretty good at math. What went wrong?"

"Well," said Brother, "it was a surprise quiz, and I've been pretty busy lately. You know there's football practice and the chess team. And I'm cramming for the quiz bowl."

"Do you think that maybe you're trying to do a little too much?" asked Papa.

"But I'm going for the All-Around Cub award this year and—"

"That's a fine goal," said Papa. "But if this paper is any sign, you might end up being the All-Around Washout. What would you think of that?"

Just then the phone rang. Papa reached for it.

"Saved by the bell," Sister whispered to Brother.

"Phew!" he said.

"Why, hello, Professor," Papa said. He sounded surprised.

Sister said, "It must be Professor Actual Factual. I wonder what he's calling about."

"Beats me," said Brother.

Professor Actual Factual was Bear Country's leading scientist. He was also the head of the famous Bearsonian Institution. He was a good friend of the Bear family. But he didn't telephone the Bears—or anyone—very often. He was much too busy with his studies and experiments at the museum. So Papa and the rest of the family were quite surprised when he called.

"Hmm," Papa said into the telephone. "Yes, Professor, I see. Of course. Brother and Sister will be glad to help. You can count on us, Professor. Good night."

Mama and the cubs were almost exploding with curiosity as Papa hung up. "Well, what was that about?" they asked all together.

Papa scratched his head. He looked a bit puzzled. "Dear, did you know that Actual Factual has a brother?" he asked Mama.

"No," she said. She raised her eyebrows. "And?"

"And the brother has a wife and a son," said Papa.

"And?" said Mama.

"And both the brother and his wife are scientists. They work in faraway places and dig up stuff."

"And that's why Actual Factual called—just to tell us that?" asked Mama.

"No," said Papa. "It seems the brother and his wife are going far away on a 'dig.' And they have sent their son to live with Actual Factual for a while. Little Ferdinand—his nickname is Ferdy—will be going to Bear Country School. The professor wants Brother and Sister to introduce him around school."

"You can do that, can't you?" Mama asked the cubs.

"Sure," said Brother. "We'll pick him up tomorrow morning on the way to school."

"Thanks, cubs," said Papa with a smile. "Professor Actual Factual has done so many good things for Bear Country over the years. It will be nice to have a chance to help him out."

Chapter 2
A Walk on the Nerdy Side

The next morning, Brother and Sister stopped by Cousin Fred's house first to pick him up. Then the three cubs headed for the Bearsonian Institution.

Professor Actual Factual and his nephew were just coming out the front door when the cubs arrived. The professor waved to them and hurried down the path. He didn't seem to notice that his nephew was taking his own good time in following.

To the cubs, little Ferdy looked like a smaller version of his uncle. He wore thick glasses, a tweed knicker suit, a maroon cap, a turtleneck, and leggings.

"Hello, cubs," said the professor. "I would like you to meet my nephew, Ferdinand Factual. Ferdy, I'd like you to meet your new friends, Brother, Sister, and Cousin—" The professor stopped speaking when he saw that Ferdy was still only halfway up the path. "Please excuse Ferdy," he whispered. "Perhaps he's a bit nervous about meeting you."

The BEARSONIAN
INSTITUTION

But as they watched Ferdy get closer, the cubs didn't think he looked a bit nervous. He walked slowly, with his hands in his pockets and a bored look on his face. The cubs could see Ferdy was in no great hurry to meet them.

"Ferdy," said Actual Factual again once his nephew reached them. "I'd like you to meet Brother, Sister, and their cousin Fred." The cubs each gave Ferdy a big smile. Then they put out their hands to shake. Ferdy's hands stayed right where

they were—in his jacket pockets. And he kept right on looking bored.

"Which of you is which?" he asked. He looked coolly from one cub to another.

"This is Sister, this is Brother, and I'm Fred," answered Cousin Fred.

"Well, shall we get on with it?" said Ferdy. He looked down the road. "I'm most curious about the 'school experience.'"

The four continued on their way to school. Sister asked Ferdy what he had meant about being curious about the "school experience."

"Oh, I've never been to school in my life," said Ferdy.

"My goodness!" cried Sister. "You're going to need a lot of help with everything: reading, writing, math—"

"Oh, my parents taught me all that when I was half your age," said Ferdy. "They're top scientists, you know. Father is a paleontologist and Mother is an archaeologist. I'm sure they are better teachers than you could find in any *school*." He said the last word as if it meant something totally worthless. "Do you know what a paleontologist is?"

Cousin Fred started to answer. One of his hobbies was reading the dictionary for fun. So of course he knew what a paleontologist was.

But Ferdy held up a hand and said, "I asked Sister." Brother looked at Ferdy. He could tell that the new cub was trying to embarrass her.

Sister frowned. She thought hard for a moment. "Pail-ee-on-tol-o-gist," she said. "Someone who makes pails?"

Ferdy smiled for the first time since the

cubs had met him. Then he threw back his
head and laughed out loud. "Ha-ha-ha!" he
roared. Tears formed in his eyes. "Someone
who makes pails! That's priceless! And I
suppose an ark-ee-ol-o-gist is someone who
makes ships? He-he-he!" He wiped his eyes.
"I guess you haven't learned those words in
school yet. Right?"

"Paleontologist: a scientist who studies
fossils," said Cousin Fred. He sounded
angry. "And an archaeologist is someone who

finds and studies artifacts from the past."

Ferdy looked surprised. "Not bad," he said to Fred. "What's your IQ?"

Fred shrugged. "I'm not sure. What's yours?"

"Oh, you're better off not knowing," said Ferdy, yawning. Then he added, "It's off the charts."

Sister didn't like being laughed at. Not one bit. She was about to tell Ferdy so. But she remembered she was supposed to be helping the professor. So she smiled and said, "Which one of your parents makes the fossils?"

"*Studies* fossils," said Ferdy. "As I already said, that's Father. And what does *your* father do?"

"He's a carpenter," answered Sister proudly. "He makes tables and chairs and stuff."

"Oh?" Ferdy chuckled. He looked down his nose at Sister. "What is his specialty: tables, chairs, or *stuff*?"

Brother was so angry at Ferdy for making fun of Papa that he stopped and grabbed Ferdy's arm. "My papa's good at *everything!*" he snapped.

The bored look on Ferdy's face didn't change. "Would you mind letting go of my arm, Brother?" he said coolly. "There is no need to be uncivilized."

"Sorry," Brother mumbled. He let go.

"Let's just drop the subject."

Ferdy arched his eyebrows. "So you don't want to talk about your father. Then what about your mother? What does she do?"

"Never mind," said Brother. He started walking again.

But Sister was determined to put in a good word for Mama. She thought about the many things Mama did. She knew they were all wonderful things, but somehow she felt that Ferdy wouldn't agree. Suddenly she had an idea. "She's a *quiltologist!*" said Sister.

Brother and Cousin Fred couldn't believe their ears. A sly smile slowly started at the corners of Ferdy's mouth. Ferdy looked at Sister. "Oh, I see," he said. "Now don't tell me—let me guess. Quiltologist. Hmm. I suppose you would think that that would be someone who makes quilts. Am I right?"

Sister stared straight ahead. With her jaw set, she nodded firmly.

Ferdy howled with laughter. "A quilt-ologist! Ha-ha-ha! Priceless!"

Sister was angry. So were Brother and Cousin Fred. Hmm, they thought. Being nice to this cub was going to be easier said than done. But Ferdy's laughter had died down. He had seen something in the distance.

"Excuse me a moment," he said. He took

a small notebook and pen from his pocket. "I am most interested in Bear Country's flora and fauna." He hurried ahead. Then he began making notes in his little book.

The cubs slowed down. They walked well behind Ferdy. "I don't know anyone named Flora or Fauna," said Sister. "Who is he talking about?"

"'Flora' means plants and 'fauna' means animals," said Cousin Fred.

Brother shook his head and made a face. "Is this cub for real? What a nerd!"

"He's more than a nerd," said Sister. "He's a big pain!"

"He's more than that," said Cousin Fred. "He's the most stuck-up cub I've ever met! That's what bothers me—not that he's smart."

Cousin Fred, a math and science whiz,

had been called a nerd a few times himself. So he really didn't like all this nerd talk.

"Just because he's smart is no reason to dislike him," he told Brother.

"You're right," said Brother. "It's the way he acts that gets to me, not his smarts."

"But we've still got to look out for him," said Sister. "We promised the professor."

Bear Country School was in sight now. Brother looked ahead. Too-Tall Grizzly and his gang were standing in their usual place in front of the school entrance.

"I'm afraid Ferdy's going to need a lot of looking out for," Brother said.

Chapter 3
Ferdy Meets Too-Tall

The Too-Tall gang liked to stand in front of the school entrance because that's where they could make the most trouble. That's what they were doing when Brother, Sister, and Fred brought Ferdy to school—making trouble. They were tripping cubs, throwing spitballs, and grabbing girls' hats and tossing them into trees.

Lately the gang had been acting up more than usual. The cubs figured it was because Too-Tall was trying to impress Queenie McBear. Everyone knew he had a major crush on her!

As Ferdy walked toward the gang, Too-Tall looked over at Queenie and turned to Skuzz, his right-hand cub. "Hey," he said, "get a load of what's coming down the road."

"Oh, boy," said Skuzz. His eyes lit up. "This is gonna be *fun*."

Ferdy was supposed to report to the school office. But he couldn't get in. The Too-Tall gang was blocking the entrance. "Well, well," said Too-Tall. He looked down at Ferdy. "If it isn't a visitor from the planet Nerd!"

The gang howled with laughter. Cubs began to gather around to see what was going on. Ferdy just looked up at Too-Tall with his normal bored expression.

"He's Actual Factual's nephew and his name is Ferdy," said Brother. "He has to report to the office, so you'd better get out of the way."

Too-Tall glanced over his shoulder at the row of gang members behind him. "Get out of the way for Nerdy Ferdy?" He laughed. "You've got to be kidding!"

"Who is this individual?" Ferdy asked Brother calmly.

"Who're you calling an *individual?*" asked Too-Tall.

WHO'RE YOU CALLING AN INDIVIDUAL?

"His name is Too-Tall," said Sister to Ferdy. "And he's bad news."

Ferdy took out his notebook and began writing in it. Too-Tall frowned. "What are you writing, Nerdy Ferdy?"

Without looking up, Ferdy said, "Not that it's any of your business, but it's my practice to make notes on local fauna."

"What's 'fauna'?" asked Too-Tall suspiciously.

"'Fauna' means animal life," said Sister. That made Queenie laugh.

"Why, that creepy little nerd," growled Too-Tall.

Queenie folded her arms across her cheerleader sweater. She winked at Ferdy. "I think he's kind of cute," she said sweetly.

"Oh, yeah?" said Too-Tall. Finally he stepped aside to let the cubs pass. "We'll see how cute he is after me and the gang get through with him at recess."

Ferdy kept taking notes as they made their way to the office. Suddenly he pointed to the school's trophy case. "What are these strange artifacts?" he asked.

"What's 'artifacts'?" asked Sister.

"Artifact," said Cousin Fred. "A made object; product of a culture or civilization."

"This is the school's trophy case," Brother said proudly. "And these are the trophies won by the school sports teams."

All at once Brother had an idea. Maybe he could talk Ferdy into joining the school's quiz-bowl team. That way Ferdy would feel more as if he belonged. And it would take some pressure off Brother. But even before Brother could open his mouth, Ferdy spoiled the thought.

"Ah, yes, sports," he said. "The opiate of the mindless."

"Opiate," said Cousin Fred. "Anything that dulls the brain . . ."

"Never mind!" said Brother. He clenched his fists. "I know an insult when I hear one!" He turned angrily to his new "friend." But Ferdy had already entered the school office to enroll.

Chapter 4
Who or Whom?

Ferdy Factual was placed in Teacher Bob's class with Brother, Cousin Fred, Queenie, and Too-Tall and his gang. As Ferdy took his seat in the back row, Teacher Bob asked him if he had reported to the office yet.

"Of course," said Ferdy. "I would never have entered the school without having first presented myself at the office."

"I see," said Teacher Bob. "Who did you talk to?"

"*Whom* did you talk to," Ferdy corrected.

There was a mixture of gasps, groans, and laughter from the other pupils. Teacher Bob looked at his new student and smiled to himself. He could see that this cub was going to be difficult.

"You're right, of course, Ferdy," he said in a friendly voice. "'Whom' is correct." Then he turned to the class and said, "Can anyone tell me why 'whom' is correct?"

Brother raised his hand and was called on. "Because it is the object of the preposition," he said.

"Very good," said Teacher Bob.

Ferdy rolled his eyes and said, "Oh, that was a toughie."

But Teacher Bob wasn't finished. Ferdy still needed to be shown who was in charge. "But when I asked Ferdy that question," he went on, "I was speaking in the vernacular."

He turned to the blackboard and wrote VER-NAC-U-LAR. "Does anyone know what 'vernacular' means?"

Cousin Fred's hand shot up. "Vernacular: the speech or language of a place; the plain language in daily use by ordinary people."

Ferdy mumbled something about "ordinary, stupid people."

Teacher Bob pretended not to hear what Ferdy had said. "I'll put it to you this way, Ferdy," he said. "Don't you agree that 'who' is all right for everyday use, even in a classroom?"

"Yes, I suppose so," said Ferdy. "Now may we get on with whatever it is you do here?"

Again, the other pupils gasped and groaned. But this time there wasn't much laughter.

Somehow, Teacher Bob kept his temper.

He had had pupils like Ferdy before. He knew all about super-smart cubs who had trouble getting along with the other cubs. He decided to work hard to make Ferdy feel comfortable. But he knew it wouldn't be easy. Ferdy already seemed to be the toughest case that he had ever seen.

Brother Bear felt sick about Ferdy's bad behavior. I could kill that little pill, he thought.

Chapter 5
Recess Rowdies

Teacher Bob tried hard to help Ferdy feel more like a member of the class. But he had little luck. Making Ferdy feel at home was not an easy job.

By the time recess rolled around, Ferdy had found four errors in his textbooks. And he had corrected the teacher's grammar three more times.

Teacher Bob was almost ready to give up on Ferdy. And the class was completely fed up with him.

At recess, Brother and Cousin Fred were so disgusted with him that they were tempted to leave Ferdy to deal on his own with Too-Tall and his gang.

"That may be what he deserves," said

Brother. But all the same, he and Cousin
Fred searched for Ferdy on the playground.
"We promised Actual Factual that we would
look out for Ferdy, so that's what we're going
to do," said Brother.

Just then he spied Ferdy and stopped.
"Uh-oh. It's worse than I thought," he said.

Ferdy was walking along with Queenie McBear. As the two walked and talked, Ferdy wrote in his notebook. Queenie seemed to be hanging on his every word.

"Wow," said Cousin Fred. "Who would have thought that Queenie would go for a nerd—er, I mean a stuck-up jerk—like Ferdy?"

"Give me a break, Fred," said Brother. "She doesn't really like Ferdy. I don't even know if she really likes Too-Tall. I think she's just trying to make trouble so she can sit back and enjoy the fireworks."

"Speaking of fireworks," said Fred, "here come Too-Tall and the gang now."

Too-Tall and his gang were headed

straight for Ferdy. They couldn't miss him. He stuck out like a sore thumb, with his strange clothes and red-framed glasses. He especially stuck out next to Queenie. She was one of the coolest cubs in the whole school.

"Hey, nerd, what'd you write about me in that stupid book?" growled Too-Tall. He grabbed the notebook from Ferdy. "Hey, here's my name!" he said. "'Too-Tall: *Schoolyardus bullyus.*' What's that supposed to mean?"

"*Schoolyardus bullyus* is the scientific name for schoolyard bully," said Ferdy. He was acting cool as a cucumber.

"Oh, yeah?" said Too-Tall. At the same time, Skuzz sneaked around behind Ferdy and crouched down. All of a sudden Too-Tall's big hands shot out. He hit Ferdy smack in the chest. Ferdy went flying backward over Skuzz.

Ferdy picked himself up. He clenched his small fists at his sides. "Give me my book!" he yelled in a high voice. But another gang member was already kneeling behind him. Too-Tall simply pushed Ferdy to the ground again. The whole gang roared with laughter.

Brother darted in. He tried to grab the notebook from Too-Tall. But the bully pulled it away. Then Too-Tall and his gang began playing monkey-in-the-middle. Brother, Cousin Fred, and Ferdy jumped again and again for the stolen book.

Suddenly Teacher Bob showed up. "All

right, knock it off!" he yelled. The game broke up and the book landed in Teacher Bob's hands. He gave the gang an angry look. "All of you, five laps around the track!" he ordered. "Get going!"

The gang took their time going. But they went. "Nerdy Ferdy, teacher's pet!" they called as they laughed and trotted off to the track.

Queenie walked up to Ferdy and batted her long eyelashes at him. "*Schoolyardus bullyus*—say, that's pretty cute," she said. Then she saw that Too-Tall was watching her from the track. She brushed the dust off Ferdy with a great show of care.

Most cubs would have been very upset

SCHOOLYARDUS BULLYUS. SAY—THAT'S PRETTY CUTE.

by what happened at recess. But it was hard to tell what Ferdy was feeling. He just got even more stuck-up than before.

During math, he went through the textbook and wrote down mistakes on a piece of paper. Then he put the paper up on the class bulletin board.

Later, during a geography lesson on Bear Country, Ferdy went over to the big wall map and corrected the names of two rivers that he said were wrong.

Finally, Teacher Bob gave the class their homework. Ferdy closed his book and pretended to fall asleep. He made loud snoring noises.

Teacher Bob could have punished Ferdy

for his bad behavior. But he knew that the class had already given him a hard enough time. He knew that they had nicknamed him "Nerdy Ferdy." And he knew that that nickname would be hard to shake.

Cousin Fred was especially angry with Ferdy. He was afraid that the stuck-up little genius would give nerds a bad name.

Brother Bear wasn't quite sure how to feel about Ferdy. Half of him felt angry. But the other half felt sorry for the little twerp.

Brother, Sister, and Cousin Fred walked Ferdy home in silence. Brother made up his mind to invite Ferdy to join the quiz-bowl team. "It would be a favor to me," he told Ferdy. "You would really help our team. You would be great."

Ferdy looked back down the street toward school. He yawned as if he were bored. "I'll put it on my list of things to think over," he said. "It will probably be a while before I let you know, though. It won't be high on the list."

Steaming, Brother turned on his heels and headed home.

Chapter 6
The Last Angry Cub

That evening, after dinner, Mama Bear called Brother and Sister into the living room. "I want to ask you something before you start your homework," she said. She sat down on the sofa. Papa sat listening in his easy chair. "How is Operation Ferdy going?"

"Oh, boy," groaned Brother, rolling his eyes. "I don't even want to talk about it."

"Me neither," said Sister.

"Oh, dear," said Mama. "It's that bad?"

The cubs nodded.

"Ferdy is having trouble fitting in?" Mama asked.

"You could say that," said Sister. "But it would be like saying a skunk wouldn't be welcome in a perfume factory." Sister went on to tell about the walk to school with Ferdy that morning.

"Then at recess," added Brother, "Too-Tall and the gang really gave him a hard time. And later on in class, Ferdy acted

ALL THE CUBS HATE HIM. NOW I HATE HIM TOO.

more stuck-up than ever. I felt sorry for him, so I invited him to join the quiz-bowl team. But he turned me down cold! He acted as if it wasn't even worth thinking about. All the cubs hate him. Now *I* hate him too."

"Me too!" added Sister.

"Oh, dear!" said Mama. "This sounds serious. Come on up here, you two." The cubs climbed up on the sofa to sit beside her.

"I'm glad you noticed how Ferdy's behavior got worse after the problems at recess," Mama said. "Do you know what that makes me think? It makes me think Ferdy had trouble getting along with other cubs even before he came to stay with his uncle."

"That can't be true," said Sister.

"Oh? Why not?" asked Mama.

"Because he's never *been* with any other cubs," said Brother.

"Surely at school . . . ," said Mama.

"He's never *been* to school," said Brother. "His parents take him on digs and things. They teach him themselves. He knows a lot. He's very smart. You know how smart Cousin Fred is. Well, Ferdy is so smart that he makes Cousin Fred look like me!"

"I think that I'm starting to understand," said Mama. "Getting along with others is something you have to learn. But Ferdy has never been around other cubs. So he has never had a chance to learn."

"But we were *nice* to him," said Sister. "Why was he so mean to us? It was only Too-Tall and his gang who gave him a hard time. Brother and Fred stood up for him. He didn't even say thanks."

"Well," said Mama. "I'm afraid some cubs are like that. Some grownups are too. It's hard to explain why. It's as if they are afraid that no one will want to be friends with them. So they don't even try making friends. That way they feel safe. That way they think their feelings won't get hurt.

"Usually they think they're not as good as others in some way. They may not be as popular. Or they may not be as good at sports. So they try to make up for it by acting like a know-it-all.

"Whenever their feelings do get hurt, they feel angry at the whole world. And they get pretty lonely that way. After a while they start to feel like the last cub in the world. It sounds to me as if Ferdy is just that kind of cub."

Brother thought for a moment. Mama

was usually right about these things. But everything she had just said seemed so complicated. A second opinion won't hurt, he thought.

"What do *you* think, Papa?" Brother asked.

Papa leaned back in his easy chair. He gazed through the window. He looked into the darkness beyond the glow of the tree-house lights. "Wimpy Walter," he said softly.

"Wimpy Walter?" said Sister. "Who's Wimpy Walter?"

Papa chuckled. "Wimpy Walter was *my* Nerdy Ferdy. Many years ago, when I was a cub at Bear Country School, a new cub named Walter moved to town.

"Walter was just like the cubs your Mama describes. He was smart as a whip. But he wasn't any good at sports. And he was afraid that the other cubs wouldn't like him. He pushed everyone away. He did that so they wouldn't have a chance to hurt his feelings. And of course, that's just what everyone did—hurt his feelings. But he expected it. . . ." Papa's voice trailed off. He sat staring off into the night, remembering.

"So what happened?" asked Brother.

"Well, a few of us kept being nice to him because we felt sorry for him. Finally he made friends with us. And he turned out to be a pretty good guy after all. Walter McLair."

"Walter McLair?" said Brother. "Do you mean Professor McLair, who teaches bee science at the university?"

"One and the same," Papa answered.

"He's a great guy!" Brother exclaimed. "Last year he took our class on a really neat field trip. He took us to see the beehives at the university research center."

"Just goes to show you," said Papa.

"Just goes to show what?" asked Brother.

"That there's still some hope for Ferdy Factual," said Papa. "I suggest you stick with Operation Ferdy a little longer."

Before going upstairs to do his homework, Brother phoned Cousin Fred to compare notes. It turned out that Fred had gotten the same sort of advice from his parents. The cubs agreed not to throw Ferdy to the wolves just yet.

Chapter 7

How Do I Love Thee?
Let Me Count the Angles

The next morning, Brother, Sister, and Cousin Fred each took a deep breath as they headed off to pick up Ferdy on the way to school. They had decided that no matter how mean Ferdy was to them, they would not be mean back to him.

But when Ferdy walked out the door of the Bearsonian Institution, the cubs saw that for once he didn't have his usual bored expression. In fact, he had a big smile on his face. He walked toward the cubs with a spring in his step.

"Good morning," Ferdy said in a pleasant voice. "How are you three today?"

The cubs looked at each other. They had puzzled looks on their faces. Brother shrugged and said, "Fine, I guess."

"Glad to hear it," said Ferdy. "Well, shall we get on with it?"

Ferdy even whistled a happy tune as they strolled down the street toward school. The cubs kept looking at each other and shrugging.

What in the world had brought about such a great change in Ferdy? At first no one could figure it out. But they finally had a clue when Brother mentioned that he had had trouble with some of his geometry homework.

"You're not the only one," said Ferdy. He chuckled.

"You did too?" asked Brother. He couldn't believe his ears.

"Oh, not I," said Ferdy. "I was thinking of Queenie McBear."

"How do you know?" asked Sister.

"She phoned me last night. She wanted to tell me how smart and interesting I am. Then she happened to mention she was having trouble with a homework problem— with five of them, to tell the truth. I'd already zipped through them right after school. So I helped her with them. She was *most* grateful. She's a very sweet girl, that Queenie. . . ."

Ferdy seemed to be getting lost in some beautiful daydream. Then he suddenly snapped out of it. He pulled a great-looking pair of binoculars out of his briefcase and peered through them at a maple tree up the road.

"What is it?" asked Sister.

"Yellow-bellied sapsucker," said Ferdy. "It might be the only one left this late in the year." He lowered his binoculars. Cousin Fred stared at them as if he wished he had a pair.

"Bearsonian property," said Ferdy. "You see, Uncle Actual has put me to work on the fall bird count. He made me an offer I couldn't refuse." Ferdy winked. "A fellow needs extra cash if he's going to take on a steady girlfriend, you know." He handed his briefcase to Cousin Fred. "Would you hold this for me, old chap? I need to make a close-up identification. I'll be back in a moment."

"We'll catch up with you," called Brother. Ferdy headed toward the maple tree.

"Girlfriend?" said Sister. "Who is he talking about?"

"Queenie, for sure," said Cousin Fred.

"But Queenie doesn't really like him. She was just trying to get the homework answers," Sister said. "If she really had a crush on him, she would at least have asked

him over to help her. She wouldn't have just asked him on the phone."

Brother nodded sadly. "*I* know that. *You* know that. And *Cousin Fred* knows that. But Ferdy doesn't have a clue."

"You would think somebody as smart as Ferdy would see through Queenie," said Sister.

"Maybe so," said Brother. "But yellow-bellied sapsuckers are one thing, and girls are another."

"And that's just what Queenie knows the little sap is," said Sister. "A sucker!"

Ferdy walked back to the cubs. He still had a dopey grin on his face.

"Look at him," said Brother. "The poor fool has fallen head over heels in love."

"Yup," said Sister. "He's in nerd heaven."

"Hey, Sis! Watch that nerd talk," said Brother. He glanced over at Cousin Fred.

"Yeah! Watch it!" said Cousin Fred, smiling.

It was all very amusing. And it was nice to see the big change that had come over Ferdy. But Brother, Sister, and Cousin Fred knew one thing for sure. If Ferdy kept making eyes at Queenie, he was headed for trouble—BIG trouble.

Chapter 8
An Uplifting Demonstration

Ferdy did keep making eyes at Queenie that morning in class. He sat in the back of the room. And Queenie kept turning around to give him the chance. Too-Tall saw all the goo-goo eyes going on. So by mid-morning he was steaming. Then came the clincher.

Suddenly Ferdy raised his hand. Brother and Cousin Fred held their breath. Until that point Ferdy hadn't said a word. The cubs had been hoping that his new mood would make Operation Ferdy a little easier.

"Yes, Ferdy?" said Teacher Bob.

"I'd very much like to deliver my report on simple machines this morning," said Ferdy.

"But it isn't due until next week," said Teacher Bob.

"Well, I had a few extra minutes last

night. And science happens to be a special interest of mine," said Ferdy cheerfully.

"Well, we do have some time now," said the teacher. He checked his watch. "Come on up to the board, Ferdy."

Queenie's smiles lifted Ferdy's spirits. He gave a bang-up report. And for once he didn't act stuck-up or snooty. Instead, he gave an interesting and lively report.

He covered five simple machines: the wedge, the inclined plane, the wheel and axle, the pulley, and the lever.

WEDGE

INCLINED PLANE

WHEEL + AXLE

PULLEY

At first the other cubs thought Ferdy was just showing off again. But soon it became clear that Ferdy was really enjoying sharing his knowledge with them.

Ferdy finally showed the power of the lever by lifting the classroom piano. He used a book as a fulcrum and the classroom window pole as a lever. The whole class was really impressed and broke into a great round of applause. Queenie clapped louder and longer than anyone else. Then she winked at Ferdy as he walked past her to his seat.

"Things are really looking up for Ferdy," Cousin Fred whispered to Brother.

Brother glanced over at Too-Tall, who was making nasty faces at Ferdy. "Yeah," he said. "Until recess, anyway."

HEY! YOU'RE SUPPOSED TO BE WATCHING FERDY!

Chapter 9
All in Fun

Brother and Cousin Fred had agreed to take turns keeping an eye on Ferdy at recess. Today it was Fred's turn. Brother warned him that Too-Tall would probably pull some really mean trick on Ferdy. So Cousin Fred promised to call Brother as soon as he saw anything suspicious going on.

A few minutes later, Brother was shooting baskets with Barry Bruin when Cousin Fred walked up smiling.

"Hey," said Brother. "You're supposed to be watching Ferdy!"

"I just came to tell you everything's

cool," said Fred. "Too-Tall doesn't seem to be going after Ferdy at all. In fact, I just heard him ask Queenie to invite Ferdy into the dodgeball game. You can never tell with Too-Tall. Sometimes he's a rat and sometimes he's okay."

"'Rat' is right," said Brother. "And I smell one. Come on!"

They raced to the dodgeball court. They pushed their way through the crowd of shouting cubs standing around it. Sure enough, there was Ferdy in his baggy

knickers. He was standing in the middle of the dodgeball circle. And he was grinning like a fool. He didn't see that the Too-Tall gang was pushing the throwers aside to take their places.

"Go, Ferdy!" yelled Queenie from the crowd.

Ferdy turned to grin at her. But at that moment Too-Tall threw the heavy dodgeball. It hit Ferdy right in the kneecap with a THWACK! Then it bounced toward another gang member. Ferdy's face twisted with pain. He grabbed his knee and began hopping around the dodgeball circle.

SMACK!

The other dodgers in the circle saw what was going on. So they quickly got out of the way.

SMACK! The ball hit Ferdy's backside and rolled away. The crowd shrieked with laughter.

"Yow!" cried Ferdy. He had one hand on his knee and the other on his backside. Now Too-Tall had the ball again.

WHACK!

"Hang in there, Nerdy Ferdy!" he laughed. "It's all in fun!" Too-Tall grinned wickedly. Then he threw hard at the back of Ferdy's head.

WHACK! Ferdy's hat and glasses flew off. He fell flat on the ground.

When Ferdy looked up, he hardly seemed to notice the crowd laughing. He couldn't take his eyes off Queenie. She was laughing so hard that tears streamed down her face.

Brother and Cousin Fred rushed over to Ferdy. But he pushed them angrily away.

"Leave me alone!" he screamed. Then he grabbed his glasses and cap, and he ran from the playground.

Chapter 10
If I Had a Lever

Brother and Cousin Fred understood how Ferdy felt. He needed to be left alone. They didn't follow him from the playground. But when they went back into the classroom after recess to take a quiz in astronomy, they had a surprise. Ferdy wasn't there.

"Where is he?" asked Fred. He looked around. "Astronomy is his favorite subject."

"He's gone," said Brother. Quietly he told Teacher Bob what had happened during recess. And just when things had begun to look up for Ferdy. Now it looked like he was missing. Teacher Bob called the school office. He told the secretary that Ferdy was missing. The secretary called Professor Actual Factual. But she couldn't reach him. So finally she called the police.

By the end of the school day, Police Chief Bruno had put together a search party. Papa and Mama Bear volunteered to search the eastern part of the forest. They picked Brother and Sister up from school and sped down the highway toward the forest.

"Wow," said Sister. "This is getting to be like one of those soap operas on TV."

"But this is the real thing," said Papa. He

shook his head. "Makes me think of Wimpy Walter. I remember the time a cub sneaked up behind him and pulled down his swimming trunks. Poor Wimpy disappeared into the forest for two days."

"Who rescued him?" asked Brother.

"He was found by Yours Truly. But I didn't exactly rescue him," said Papa. "In fact, *he* sort of rescued *me*—from a swarm of angry bees when I stumbled into their hive. Hmm . . . maybe that led to his interest in bee science!"

Soon they reached the edge of the forest and piled out of the car. "I'll go search Forbidden Bog," Papa told Mama. "It's too dangerous for you and the cubs."

Mama looked worried, but she nodded. "We'll search the lakefront," she said. Papa vanished among the trees. "Now be careful, dear. . . ."

The lake was still and glassy under the late afternoon sun. The silence of the forest was broken only by birdsong and the chattering of squirrels.

At first Mama and the cubs found no sign of anyone. But then Sister saw a small figure far across the lake.

"I'll bet it's Ferdy," she said. She peered into the distance. "It seems to be dressed like him."

But when they reached the other side of the lake, they found Professor Actual Factual standing there instead. He was studying a row of test tubes he had placed along the shore.

"Why, hello, folks!" he said with a smile. "What a pleasant surprise!"

"What are you doing here?" they asked. "Are you also looking for—"

"Oh, yes," he said. "I'm looking for phytoplankton—"

"Fight-o-*what?*" asked Sister.

"Never mind that, Sister!" said Brother.

"Please listen, Professor," said Mama. "Your nephew Ferdy is missing!"

"Missing?" said the professor. "What is he missing?"

"Please, Professor," said Brother. *"It's Ferdy that's missing! He's gone! Nowhere to*

be found! Missing!"

"Oh, my goodness!" said the professor. "Come! We must find him!"

"We're looking everywhere for him," said Mama. "Papa went to look for him in Forbidden Bog."

"Oh, dear!" said the professor. He raised a hand to his mouth. "There's a big patch of quicksand in that bog! He may not know about it!"

"Don't worry, Professor," said Sister. "I'm sure Ferdy knows quicksand when he sees it."

"Actually," said the professor, "it wasn't Ferdy I was thinking of. It was Papa!"

Off they hurried to Forbidden Bog. Professor Actual Factual led the way. He seemed to know every narrow trail. He seemed to know every thornbush and every foothold in the rocks.

THWOCK!

Mama and the cubs followed close behind. "The quicksand is just up ahead," the professor said at last.

Suddenly they heard a small voice cry, "Hold on!" Then they heard a giant THWOCK! It sounded like a heavy object being pulled out of a huge pot of day-old oatmeal. In another moment they were at the clearing.

There was Papa Bear. He was coated with muck and hanging on to a strong branch. Ferdy had made a lever from the fallen branch. Then he made a fulcrum from a rock. He used the two of them to rescue Papa from the patch of quicksand.

Ferdy lifted and lowered Papa to solid ground. The would-be hero lay there, gasping for breath.

THWOCK!

Once his rescue job was done, Ferdy saw that his uncle and the Bears were standing beside him. He turned to them with a proud grin and said, "As the ancient Greek scientist said, 'Give me a lever and a place to stand and I can move the world.'"

"Very fine work, Ferdy!" cried Actual Factual. "Are you all right, Papa Bear?"

"All right?" said Papa. "Of course I'm all right. It takes more than a little mud to hurt *me*."

"It's not mud," said Mama. "It's *quick-sand*."

"I was sitting here taking some notes on it," Ferdy said. "I tried to warn him. But he ran right into it."

"I thought Ferdy was in trouble," said Papa. "This bog is a dangerous place for a cub."

Chapter 11
Abuse a Nerd, Get Suspended

The news of how Ferdy had rescued Papa Bear spread quickly through Bear Country. It did wonders for Ferdy's popularity.

Ferdy had shown the other cubs that being smart was useful for more than homework. It was useful even in matters of life and death. Ferdy's whole mood changed. He felt so good that he even agreed to join the quiz-bowl team.

"I've been brushing up on my trigonometry, calculus, cytology, microbiology, biochemistry, quantum physics, and a few other subjects," he told Brother as they

walked home from school one afternoon. "I assume we'll do quite well in the quiz bowl next week."

Brother walked along without looking up. "Sure," he mumbled. "With you on the team, it'll be a cinch to win the trophy."

"What's the matter? You don't seem very happy about it," said Ferdy.

"Oh, I am. I am," said Brother. He sighed. "It's the football team I'm unhappy about."

As they walked along, Ferdy wondered if he should ask Brother more about his football problems. He knew nothing about football. And he didn't want Brother to know that there was something he knew nothing about. But Brother seemed so unhappy. He seemed so worried. Maybe there was something Ferdy could do to help.

"What seems to be the problem?" Ferdy finally asked.

Brother told Ferdy how Too-Tall Grizzly had been suspended from the team as punishment for leading the dodgeball attack on him.

"And we're up against the Bruin City Bulldogs this weekend," Brother added glumly. "They beat us pretty badly last year. Too-Tall is our top-notch tight end. Without him we haven't got a chance."

Ferdy thought for a moment as they walked. "How about this," he said. "I'll go to

the principal and ask to have Too-Tall put back on the team. The whole mess started over me, anyway, and—"

"But I thought you hated Too-Tall," Brother said. He sounded surprised.

"It isn't just Too-Tall we're talking about here," said Ferdy. "It's the whole football team. And the football team plays for the school. So logically speaking, it's the whole school we're talking about."

"Gee," said Brother. "It takes a pretty together cub to see the big picture like that."

"Well, it's not just the big picture," said Ferdy. "It's also the little picture."

"How do you mean?"

"Yesterday at recess I happened to overhear Queenie. She was breaking up with Too-Tall. She told him off for getting suspended. Then she told him that if the football team got creamed again by the

Bulldogs, she would be terribly embarrassed. That's because she's head cheerleader. Then she called him a big, stupid klutz."

"So now you and Too-Tall have something in common!" said Brother. He was thinking of the sneaky way Queenie had used them against each other.

"Yes," said Ferdy. "I'm afraid I was wrong about Queenie."

"*You*—wrong about something?" said Brother. Of course he was teasing.

"Why not?" said Ferdy. He sounded serious. "I'm planning to be a scientist, you

know. A scientist must learn to recognize error—even his own."

"Well," said Brother. "That's an interesting way to look at it. Weird, but interesting."

"So, you see, I really want to go to the principal."

"It's very nice of you to offer," said Brother. "But Too-Tall isn't the only problem. The main problem is that Bruin City is a much bigger school with a much bigger squad. They have lots of extra players to use during a game. That wears us down."

"There must be *something* you can do," said Ferdy. They had reached the Bearsonian.

"I'm afraid you don't know much about football, Ferd," said Brother.

"No, but I can learn," said Ferdy. "Lend me your rule book. I'll study it overnight.

Maybe I can come up with something. And I'll phone the principal tonight. I hope I can talk him into putting Too-Tall back on the team. I can see that you chaps need all the help you can get against these Bulldogs."

Brother shrugged. Then he pulled his rule book from his backpack and handed it to Ferdy. Ferdy waved good-bye and headed eagerly up the path to the museum.

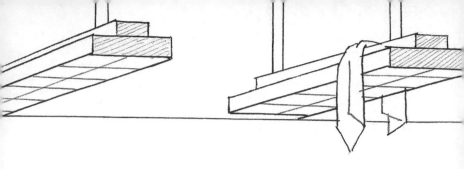

Chapter 12
Oh, to Be a Football Hero

The next day, there was a meeting before football practice. Coach Grizzmeyer was drawing plays on the locker-room blackboard when he felt a tap on his arm.

"Uh, Coach, may I have a word with you?"

The coach turned. He saw a small cub in a maroon cap and knickers looking up at him through thick glasses. Little Ferdy was a funny sight next to all the football players in their pads and uniforms. The coach almost laughed. But then he thought about what a hero Ferdy had been. And he had heard about his helpful call to the principal. "What can I do for you, Ferdy?" the coach asked.

"I have a plan for beating the Bulldogs this weekend," Ferdy said softly.

"That's a laugh," said Too-Tall Grizzly.

"Quiet down back there!" snapped Coach Grizzmeyer. "If it weren't for Ferdy, you wouldn't even be on the team, Too-Tall." The coach had a rule against being interrupted during locker-room meetings. But for Ferdy he decided he could break the rule—even if Ferdy had never touched a football in his life! "Go ahead, Ferdy," the coach said.

Ferdy turned so that he was talking to

both the coach and the players. "Let me state it in logical terms," he began. "If one assumes that the strength of the Bruin City team depends on its ability to substitute freely, then it follows that the key to beating them is to interfere with their ability to do so. Clearly, the simplest answer is to put in a 'hurry-up, no-huddle' offense. Or, as the ancient Chinese philosopher said, 'Sow confusion to the wind and you make your enemy chaff.'"

A murmur ran through the team. Coach Grizzmeyer stroked his chin. "Hmm," he said. "I don't know much about ancient Chinese philosophers. But I'll bet none of them ever read the football rule book."

"A good assumption, no doubt," said Ferdy.

"Are you sure this 'hurry-up, no-huddle' offense would be within the rules?"

"Absolutely, Coach," said Ferdy. "I have studied the entire rule book. You can be sure that it will be legal. How about putting it to a vote?"

"Why vote?" said the coach. "I'm the coach, and what I say goes. . . ." Frowning, he thought for a moment. Then his face broke into a smile. "I say we try it!"

Ferdy Factual had already won over most Bear Country cubs after rescuing Papa Bear at Forbidden Bog. Now his "hurry-up, no-huddle" offense helped him get rid of his

"Nerdy Ferdy" nickname.

The Bear Country Cousins defeated the Bruin City Bulldogs, 21–14. Too-Tall Grizzly made a great catch of a Brother Bear pass for the winning touchdown! The team tried to lift Too-Tall to their shoulders.

But Too-Tall wouldn't let them. Instead,

he called Ferdy down from the stands and lifted him to his shoulders as the true hero of the game. The crowd roared and cheered for Ferdy.

The other gang members on the team

were shocked. "But wait a minute!" said Skuzz to Too-Tall. "Why are you doing that to that no-good, stuck-up little nerd?"

"Cut it out!" Too-Tall barked. "I don't want to hear any more of that kind of talk." He reached up and patted Ferdy on the back. "The little guy can't help it if he's a genius, can he?"

Stan and Jan Berenstain began writing and illustrating books for children in the early 1960s, when their two young sons were beginning to read. That marked the start of the best-selling Berenstain Bears series. Now, with more than 95 books in print, videos, television shows, and even a Berenstain Bears theme park, it's hard to tell where the Bears end and the Berenstains begin!

Stan and Jan make their home in Bucks County, Pennsylvania, and plan on writing and illustrating many more books for children, especially for their four grandchildren, who keep them well in touch with the kids of today.